Greater Than a To Connecticut USA

50 Travel Tips from a Local

C. A. Wisniewski

Copyright © 2017 CZYK Publishing
All Rights Reserved. No part of this publication may be reproduced, including scanning and photocopying, or distributed in any form or by any means, electronic or mechanical, or stored in a database or retrieval system without prior written permission from the publisher.

Disclaimer: The publisher has put forth an effort in preparing and arranging this book. The information provided herein by the author is provided "as is". Use this information at your own risk. Consult your doctor before engaging in any medical activities. The publisher and author disclaim any liabilities for any loss of profit or commercial or personal damages resulting from the information contained in this book.

Order Information: To order this title please email lbrenenc@gmail.com or visit GreaterThanATourist.com. A bulk discount can be provided.

Cover Template Creator: Lisa Rusczyk Ed. D. using Canva.
Cover Creator: Lisa Rusczyk Ed. D.
Image: https://pixabay.com/en/squantz-pond-connecticut-landscape-209864/

CZYK
PUBLISHING

Lock Haven, PA
All rights reserved.
ISBN: 9781549629778

>TOURIST

Wisniewski

BOOK DESCRIPTION

Are you excited about planning your next trip?

Do you want to try something new?

Would you like some guidance from a local?

If you answered yes to any of these questions, then this Greater Than a Tourist book is for you.

Connecticut by C.A. Wisniewski offers the inside scoop on Connecticut. Most travel books tell you how to sightsee. Although there's nothing wrong with that, as a part of the Greater than a Tourist series, this book will give you tips from someone who lives at your next travel destination. In these pages, you'll discover local advice that will help you throughout your trip.

Travel like a local. Slow down and get to know the people and the culture of a place. By the time you finish this book, you will be eager and prepared to travel to your next destination.

Wisniewski

TABLE OF CONTENTS

BOOK DESCRIPTION

TABLE OF CONTENTS

DEDICATION

FROM THE PUBLISHER

WELCOME TO > TOURIST

INTRODUCTION

1. Planning Your Visit

2. Planning Your Stay

3. Know Where You Want To Go

4. Mingle at Mohegan Sun

5. Frolic At Foxwoods

6. Meander Through Mystic

7. Discover The Falls

8. Seek the Thrill at Lake Compounce

9. Dining at Lenny and Joe's Fish Tale

10. Wining Along The Connecticut Wine Trail

11. Appreciate Hammonasset Beach State Park

12. Explore The Niantic Bay Boardwalk

13. Eat At Bill's Seafood Restaurant

14. Reign At Gillette Castle State Park

15. Kayake, Eat, Shop, Oh My!

16. Railing on the Essex Steam Train and Riverboat

17. Spend The Day At Ocean Beach Park

18. Challenge Yourself At The It Adventure Ropes Course

19. Find Tranquility At Crescent Lake

20. Pick Your Own Fruit At Lyman Orchards

21. Devour Apple Fritters

22. Stop By The Durham Fair

23. Observe Waterfalls

24. Hike Through Sleeping Giant State Park

25. Hike To Castle Craig

26. Cruise Around The Thimble Islands

27. Sink Into The Submarine Force Library & Museum

28. Join The Animals At The Beardsley Zoo

29. Dining Outside At Goats N' Roses

30. Eat Pizza at Pepe's

31. Explore Exotic Animals At Action Wildlife

>TOURIST

32. Tour the Capitol Building

33. Stroll Through Bushnell Park

34. Shopping, Walking, And Eating At West Hartford Center

35. Lodging And Relaxing At The Madison Beach Hotel

36. Rejuvinate At The Water's Edge Resort and Spa

37. Have Fun At The Hops Company

38. Drink Beer At Stony Creek Brewery

39. Visit The Mark Twain House And Museum

40. Go Back In Time At The Dinosaur State Park

41. Walk The West Cornwall Covered Bridge

42. Dining at Fresh Salt at Saybrook Point Inn

43. Eat Gourmet Burgers And Hot Dogs Like A Local

44. Walk The Labyrinths

45. Eat, Stay, Explore At Hopkins Inn

46. Dine At Apricot's Restaurant and Pub

47. Drink, Eat, Relax On The Roof

48. Watch And Dine At 121 Restaurant At OXC

49. Drink, Party, And Pedal On The Elm City Park Bike

50. Look Forward To Seeing You

Top Reasons to Book This Trip

Wisniewski

Our Story

Notes

DEDICATION

This book is dedicated to my Goddaughter, Harper Mae. She is my inspiration to be the best person that I can be, challenging myself each day to become the best version of myself. Harper allows me to be a kid again, finding such joy in the smallest moments such as blowing bubbles, reading a book, or singing at the top of our lungs. May all who read this book have the courage to let their inner child out every once in a while.

Wisniewski

ABOUT THE AUTHOR

C.A. Wisniewski is a born and raised Connecticut resident. C.A. was born in the small suburb of Southington where she lived for 25 years. When purchasing her first home, she chose to remain in the state of Connecticut, moving a couple of towns east, to the city of New Britain.

C.A. Wisniewski graduated from Central Connecticut State University with a Bachelor's Degree in Elementary Education, and she graduated from the University of St. Joseph's with a Master's Degree in Special Education. She currently teaches third grade. C.A. Wisniewski has been an avid writer since her days as a child, and continues to enjoy writing in her spare time as an adult. She enjoys writing informational texts, poems, and inspirational articles. Right now, her goal is to bring more Mindfulness Education to today's children. Now, more than ever, society needs to reconnect with what it means to be human, civil, and centered.

Mindfulness is the tool society needs to help everyone slow down, breathe, and focus on what is important: being kind, accepting, and living in the present moment.

HOW TO USE THIS BOOK

The Greater Than a Tourist book series was written by someone who has lived in an area for over three months. The goal of this book is to help travelers either dream or experience different locations by providing opinions from a local. The author has made suggestions based on their own experiences. Please do your own research before traveling to the area in case the suggested places are unavailable.

Wisniewski

FROM THE PUBLISHER

Traveling can be one of the most important parts of a person's life. The anticipation and memories that you have are some of the best. As a publisher of the Greater Than a Tourist book series, as well as the popular 50 Things to Know book series, we strive to help you learn about new places, spark your imagination, and inspire you. Wherever you are and whatever you do I wish you safe, fun, and inspiring travel.

Lisa Rusczyk Ed. D.

CZYK Publishing

Wisniewski

>TOURIST

WELCOME TO > TOURIST

Wisniewski

INTRODUCTION

Connecticut, also known as the Nutmeg State or the Constitution State, has always been recognized for its historical impact on American society. For example, Connecticut was home to some of the most famous scholars such as Mark Twain and Noah Webster. Connecticut is also home to some of the nation's top colleges such as: the University of Connecticut and Yale University. The Mohegan Sun and Foxwoods Casinos also attract many visitors from near and far. However, Connecticut locals understand that Connecticut is so much more than that.

The state of Connecticut is a small state, where towns become like families, looking out for one another. Connecticut is so unique in that you can literally travel from one end of the state to the other in less than 2 hours. Moreover, Connecticut is rich in culture, socioeconomic statuses, and diversity. Many popular celebrities have even chosen to call Connecticut home. Katharine Hepburn, Ron Howard, and Michael Bolton have all been known to reside in Connecticut at one point in time. In addition, Connecticut has four beautiful seasons. Just when you get sick and tired of the hot weather, the brisk and cool Fall is right around the corner. Similarly, when you've had enough of the shoveling and plowing, you know Spring is right around the corner. With the changing seasons, Connecticut offers so many unique and wonderful opportunities for different times of the year. No matter the time of year, Connecticut is guaranteed to provide stunning scenic views with a wide variety of things to see and do.

1. Planning Your Visit

First and foremost, you must decide when to plan your visit. The wonderful thing about the state of Connecticut is that it is beautiful to visit any time of the year. Each season has something different and unique to offer in this great state. Autumn offers fun fairs and breathtaking foliage; while, Winter is perfect for snow filled adventures. Spring and Summer are ideal for spending time in the great outdoors, basking in the warm sun while taking in the scenic views. No matter the season, there are countless museums and landmarks to visit, things to do, and places to see.

2. Planning Your Stay

Once you decide when you are going to visit, the next

thing you must decide is where you are going to stay. One of the most unique things about the state of Connecticut is that it is so small. In less than two hours, you can travel from one side of Connecticut to the other. Therefore, it's not necessary to plan your stay around the places you wish to see and visit. With that being said, you might want to consider lodging somewhere in Central Connecticut. This way, you have fairly easy access to almost any place you'd like to go. Hartford, West Hartford, Farmington, Avon, and Simsbury are some of the most beautiful areas in Central Connecticut that offer hotels and inns for lodging. However, Connecticut's best hotels and inns are found closer to its borders. If you prefer a more exquisite and elegant stay; and you don't mind traveling a little further to your destinations, you may want to consider staying at one of these locations instead.

3. Know Where You Want To Go

Do your research in advance of your trip and have an idea as to what you want to do and what places you want to visit. This way, you can plan your trip accordingly. For example, you may consider visiting a group of vineyards in northern Connecticut on the same day. Or perhaps you'd like to stop at a beach and eat at a nearby restaurant afterwards. You will get the most out of your stay if you try to visit a variety of places in a specific location over the course of one or two days. Since Connecticut is so small, you can see and do a lot in just one day. If you know what you would like to do in advance, you'll be able to plan your trip around locations and travel times to each of your destinations. As a result, you'll have the privilege to fully enjoy your stay without worrying about where you are going to go, what you are going to do, or how long it will take to get there.

4. Mingle at Mohegan Sun

You'll definitely want to take some time to stop and mingle at the Mohegan Sun Resort and Casino in Uncasville. Uncasville is located in the southeastern region of the state. Mohegan Sun contains three main casinos: Casino of the Sky, Casino of the Earth, and Casino of the Wind. Each Casino contains unique restaurants, shops, and of course, lots of gaming opportunities. Johnny Rockets, in the Casino of the Sky, serves your typical All American food in an exciting and vibrant atmosphere. You'll enjoy listening to upbeat music and slurping delicious milkshakes as your servers dance their way to your table. Another restaurant with great food and fun ambiance is Margaritaville in the Casino of the Wind. When you first walk in, you'll notice the extraordinarily large margarita drink standing in the middle of the restaurant. Every once in a while, this margarita comes to life as Jimmy Buffet's timeless classic "Margaritaville" plays in the background. The restaurant includes multiple bars, a concert stage, and two levels of open, dining space. On the top level of the restaurant, you can enjoy open air dining as you overlook the scenic Thames River. Mohegan Sun is also well known for its vivacious and active nightlife scene. The Wolf Den, Avalon, and the VISTA Lounge are just a sample of the options where you can enjoy the casinos' after hours fun. In addition to all there is to see and do at the casinos, Mohegan Sun is also a hotel, containing a spa and golf club. If you're willing to splurge some extra money on booking your stay at Mohegan Sun, you're sure to have an experience you won't forget.

5. Frolic At Foxwoods

A couple of miles down the road from Mohegan Sun, located in Mashantucket, is a second Connecticut casino, Foxwoods

Resort and Casino. The Foxwoods Resort is actually made up of four elegant hotels: the Grand Pequot Tower, the Villas, the Grand Cedar Hotel, and the Two Trees Inn. However, Foxwoods is so much more than just its four casinos. Foxwoods is full of restaurants, shops, activities, slot machines, table games, and shows. One of the newest attractions is the Thrill Tower. Here, thrill seekers have the opportunity to freefall from the top of the Thrill Tower on the Sky Drop. On Sky Launch, riders are propelled from the ground to the top of Thrill Tower and back down again at an astronomical speed. If you would prefer a less adventurous experience, you might enjoy the shops at the Tanger Outlets, the Norwich Spa, the G Spa at Fox Tower, or Bingo. Similar to Mohegan Sun, Foxwoods also has an active and exciting nightlife. Whether you prefer to dance the night away or relax with that special someone, there is something for everyone during the nightlife scene. The Shrine Bar is one of the most popular nightlife bars. There's also fun to be had at the Hard Rock Café, the Halo Bar, and the Scorpion

Bar. No matter if you choose to lodge in one of the hotels or just spend the day, you'll definitely want to include some Foxwoods frolicking into your Connecticut trip.

6. Meander Through Mystic

Mystic is one of the most charming little towns located along the Connecticut shoreline near the Rhode Island border. Mystic is filled with things to do, attractions to see, and places to eat. One of the most notable attractions is Mystic Aquarium. A family fun adventure of aquarium exhibits such as: African Penguins, Beluga Whales, and Frogs awaits you. There's also countless species of Fish, Sea Lions, and Seals to see. You can even observe live feedings, animal acts, and enjoy a unique 4D theater experience. After an exciting day at the aquarium, you might consider walking over to the shops at Olde Mistick Village. Antiques, toys, and home décor are just some of the many treasures you'll find when exploring the shops.

    When planning your visit to Mystic, make sure you include a stop at Downtown Mystic. This historic, little village is full of unique shops, restaurants, and riverside activities. Mystic Pizza, home to the 1988 Julia Roberts movie "Mystic Pizza", is definitely a must-try. When you're not shopping, walking along the boardwalk, or eating, you can enjoy kayaking or paddle boarding along the Mystic River. You can also partake in historic harbor tours and Mystic River cruises. If you're willing to open up your wallet a little wider, there's also a handful of exquisite, quaint places of lodging to consider. In order to fully enjoy all the wonder and fun that Mystic has to offer, you should probably incorporate more than a one day's visit to this beautiful, historic town.

>TOURIST

7. Discover The Falls

Kent Falls State Park, located in Kent, is one of Connecticut's hidden gems. There is so much beauty to absorb in this park that sits along the scenic Housatonic River. If you are adventurous, you can enjoy a steep hike along the falls on the Kent Falls Trails. If you prefer a less intense activity, you can enjoy a stroll over the covered bridge or walk along the Art Trail Site. This is where you can observe outdoor exhibits that reflect 19th century art and life. The park is also a popular destination for Trout fishing as well as picnicking. Additionally, pets are welcome on hikes and walks on the trails as well as throughout the picnic areas. For your convenience, bathroom facilities, picnic tables, and grills are located throughout the park. If you're visiting on a weekend or a holiday between Memorial Day and October 31st, you will have to pay a parking fee. The fee ranges between $9.00 for state residents and $15.00 for out-of-state visitors. No matter the time of year you explore Kent Falls State Park, you're sure to encounter a stunning, natural landscape as the falls cascade around you.

8. Seek the Thrill at Lake Compounce

Lake Compounce is an amusement park located in Southington and Bristol that the whole family can enjoy. Lake Compounce is actually the oldest, continuously running amusement park in North America! Adventure seekers will definitely get their fill with roller coasters and thrill rides galore! First and foremost, the Wildcat roller coaster is a must! It may not be the scariest roller coaster that the park has to offer, but this wooden coaster has been operating for over 90 years! It's the first thing you'll see and hear as you walk into the park. You'll either hear the carts creaking up the wooden tracks or the screams of the riders as the carts drastically drop along the other side. It'll definitely get your thrill juices flowing. If you're brave enough, you'll have to try the park's newest coaster called the Phobia Phear Coaster. You'll go forwards, backwards, upside down, and inside out. Warning: don't attempt this ride on a full stomach. Of course, Boulder Dash, the world's number one wooden roller coaster, is a must as well. If roller coasters aren't your thing, there's also water rides, classic rides, and a great selection of kiddie rides. Who doesn't love a good carousel, Ferris wheel, or bumper cars? When you're not busy getting wet or seeking thrills, there's plenty of food options to choose from. Everything from Mexican to Italian and good ole All American Cuisine are located in various locations throughout the park. The park's regular season begins around Memorial Day Weekend and typically lasts until Labor Day Weekend. After that, the park is open on weekends only until the end of December. The Haunted Graveyard Attraction is open from the end of September to the end of October, and the Holiday

Lights Display is typically available throughout the weekends of the month of December. It doesn't matter when you decide to visit Lake Compounce, there will always be something exciting going on!

9. Dining at Lenny and Joe's Fish Tale

There are actually three Lenny and Joe's Fish Tale Restaurants located along Connecticut's Shoreline. The one that you should take the time to visit is found in Madison. This is the perfect place to stop after spending a day on the beach at Hammonasset State Park or after a day enjoying the outlet shops in Clinton. When you first walk into the restaurant, you're likely to embark upon a crowd of people waiting to place an order or waiting to pick up their order. Don't let the crowd of people intimidate you. The line moves very quickly. Besides, it'll give you time to look up at the menu and decide what to order. Seafood lovers must try the Hot Lobster Roll, the Fresh Fried Scrod, or the Shrimp and Scallops. Once you place your order, you can decide where you want to sit. You don't have to wait for your order in the lobby because your number will be announced over the loudspeaker when it's ready. There's indoor and outdoor seating to choose from. If the weather permits, you should take the time to enjoy the outdoor dining. Feel free to bring your own table cloth, drinks (alcoholic beverages are permitted), and cups. If you have kids with you, they'll probably want to enjoy the carousel ride after eating. If your stomach isn't too full, you'll also want to treat yourself to a delicious, soft serve ice cream. No matter what location you decide to visit, Lenny and Joe's offers the freshest seafood in a fun and laid back environment.

10. Wining Along The Connecticut Wine Trail

Wine lovers, rejoice! The Connecticut Wine Trail is just for you. The Connecticut Wine Trail connects vineyards and wineries throughout some of the most beautiful and scenic regions of the state. With over twenty wineries situated in various locations throughout the state, you'll have to be sure to incorporate a couple of stops along the Wine Trail during your stay. Gouveia Vineyards, located in the town of Wallingford, is laid across a rounding hill of woodlands, overlooking the acres of vineyards which surround you. You will enjoy some award winning wine while relaxing in the scenic outdoors or while cozying up to a fire during the colder, winter months.

Another popular vineyard, not far down the road from Gouveia, is Paradise Hills Vineyard and Winery. Much smaller than Gouveia, Paradise Hills offers a welcoming and warm, family-oriented environment. It almost feels like home when you walk inside the winery for the first time. The staff always seems to embrace its customers with open arms. After enjoying a wine tasting, you can relax in the great outdoors, either on the patio or on the grounds surrounding the vineyard. When the weather does not permit, you can kick back in the charming and cozy, little tasting room. When planning your stay, be sure to research the Connecticut Wine Trail and plan to visit some of the wineries that happen to be along your way. Or, you may just want to plan an exciting day of vineyard hopping. Just make sure to have a designated driver if this is the route you choose!

Wisniewski

>TOURIST

"Kindness is the language which the deaf can hear and the blind can see." ~Mark Twain

Wisniewski

11. Appreciate Hammonasset Beach State Park

Hammonasset Beach State Park in Madison is so much more than your typical beach. Even if you're not a beach person, you'll find something to enjoy when visiting the park. When you first drive into the park, you'll notice that it has a large, open space dedicated to camping. If you are a camper, you might want to consider spending a couple of days here during your stay. As you drive further into the park, you'll likely see people walking, jogging, biking, or roller blading. The park is actually a very popular place for people to simply enjoy some exercise or a casual stroll. As you continue your drive into the park, you'll start to see parking signs for the various beaches. With over two miles of sandy beach stretching along the coast, there are plenty of options to choose from. Two of the most popular beaches are Meigs Point and West Beach. These two beaches offer restroom facilities, showers, and concession stands. Meigs

Point also contains the Nature Center, which is another common area attraction. The Nature Center offers programs and activities year round. In addition to basking in the sun and surf or exercising, visitors can also enjoy salt water fishing, canoeing and kayaking. Whether you're camping for a couple of days or just spending a day on the beach, you'll definitely want to make sure you stay long enough to relish in the beautiful sunset. Watching the sun set along the beautiful shores of Long Island Sound is a breathtaking and wonderful experience.

12. Explore The Niantic Bay Boardwalk

The Niantic Bay Boardwalk, located in East Lyme, stretches just over a mile long against Long Island Sound. This boardwalk is the perfect place to enjoy a leisurely walk, with the beautiful, sound waters serving as the backdrop. The eastern portion of the boardwalk is composed primarily of synthetic materials, offering a legitimate "boardwalk" feel. Also along this region of the boardwalk is a white sand beach, open to the public, for swimming, picnicking, fishing, and sunbathing. Unlike the eastern portion, the west side of the boardwalk is made up of gravel and rock. You'll be able to see and hear the waves crashing against the rocky shores as you travel along this section of the boardwalk. Benches are conveniently located in various spots along the boardwalk, allowing the opportunity to simply sit and take in the beautiful surroundings.

When you're finished strolling along the boardwalk, be sure to head up to the shops and restaurants on Main Street. Main Street sits parallel to the boardwalk, and contains several unique stores and eateries. Some restaurants, such as The Main Street Grille and Sunset Ribs offer spectacular views of Long Island Sound with rooftop dining. No matter the season, these are excellent spots to observe a setting sun or the ocean wildlife in their natural habitat.

13. Eat At Bill's Seafood Restaurant

Bill's Seafood Restaurant in Westbrook is open year round. It's definitely a place you should stop when the weather permits. The restaurant is conveniently located behind the "singing bridge". To fully enjoy the Bill's experience, you should try to go at a time when you can sit on the outside deck. You won't be sitting outside for long before you understand how the "singing bridge" got its name. The outdoor dining is laid out against a causeway where boats pass through and seagulls are eagerly awaiting the next dropped French fry. Live music is also usually playing by the outdoor bar throughout the late spring and summer months. Although it's hard not to enjoy seafood when dining at this restaurant, there are plenty of other menu options for those that do not prefer seafood. If you're going to embark on seafood, you must try the Steamed Prince Edward Island Mussels or the Clam Strip Platter. Make sure you don't fill up too much, because you'll definitely want to save some room for ice cream. As you head back to your car, take time to stop at Bill's Seafood Ice Cream & Gift Shop. It is important to note that Bill's Seafood Restaurant does not accept credit cards. However, an ATM is available on site.

14. Reign At Gillette Castle State Park

Gillette Castle State Park is located in East Haddam, and is the perfect place to visit for those who enjoy history, hiking, and the outdoors. Unfortunately, the castle is only open from Memorial Day to Labor Day, so if it's a desirable place to visit, you should consider planning your Connecticut stay somewhere in between that time period. With that being said, the outdoor grounds and surrounding premises are open year round. Gillette Castle State Park is most popular for its stunning views, both on the ground level as well as the castle level. In order to get the most out of your visit to the castle, you will need to hike the trails to the hilltop where the castle stands. While the hike is not too intense, it is an incline hike and it is on natural ground, so it can be somewhat strenuous.

From the outside, the stone castle appears to be of medieval decent. However, the castle is really only traced back to the early 1900's. Once you've reached the castle, you can purchase a ticket go inside for a self-guided tour. Children and adults of all ages will enjoy learning about the history of the castle while exploring the mansion and some of its original furnishings. If you are visiting during the off-season and cannot get into the castle, you can still enjoy the miraculous views atop the Connecticut River. You can also hike various additional trails or stop to enjoy a picnic lunch. Camp grounds are also on site from the beginning of May to the end of September. In addition, a Visitor Center and Food Concessions are also located in the park.

15. Kayake, Eat, Shop, Oh My!

Collinsville is an adorable, little town tucked inside the town of Canton. Collinsville is rich in history and beauty. Collinsville was actually built around the Collins Company Axe Factory. While the factory no longer exists, the vintage charm of the village has sustained throughout the years. It's highly suggested that you explore Collinsville during the warmer months when you can fully enjoy all the recreational activities that are offered along the Farmington River. One of the most relaxing and fun activities is kayaking through Collinsville Canoe & Kayak. This particular stretch of the Farmington River is much calmer than the rest of the river, so you don't have to worry about battling white water rapids.

However, if you take your kayak far enough up the river, there's a very small area of "mini" rapids that are a fun challenge to try and navigate. Most people give up, jump out of their kayak, and push it across the rapids. Will you be brave enough to battle the rapids?

    If water sports aren't your thing, there is also the Farmington River Greenway which runs through a scenic walking/biking trail. Be sure that you also take some time to explore the village's shops and restaurants where you will get a little peak into the history that makes Collinsville so special. Collinsville is well known for its antique shops and area restaurants. For instance, the Crown & Hammer Restaurant is located inside an old, train depot. Inside a cozy and warm atmosphere, you can enjoy delicious food and live music on the weekends. You may also choose to simply enjoy a picnic along the Farmington River. Collinsville is a popular favorite of Connecticut's locals, so you'll definitely want to put it on your itinerary when visiting the state.

16. Railing on the Essex Steam Train and Riverboat

The Essex Steam Train and Riverboat experience is located in the town of Essex. The majority of the events are held between May and October, but a handful of special events run through the winter as well. A typical excursion begins at the Essex Station where you will board the steam train. The train runs at a comfortable speed of about 20 mph so that you can fully take in your surroundings as you travel through the countryside. Once you reach Deep River Landing, you will then board the Becky Thatcher Riverboat for a cruise along the Connecticut River. Similar to the train ride, the riverboat will carry you through some of Connecticut's most popular historic sites such as: The Goodspeed Opera House and Gillette Castle. You can also simply enjoy observing the beautiful landscape and the river wildlife. Upon the conclusion of the cruise, you will then board the steam train one last time, where it will take you back to the Essex Station. However, The Essex Steam Train and Riverboat is probably most popular for its various seasonal events. For example, The North Pole Express typically sells out within the first day or two of sales. Families take a magical journey aboard the steam train to the North Pole. The sunset cruises are also a common attraction for both tourists and local residents. When you are planning your Connecticut stay, you should research what will be happening on the Essex Steam Train and Riverboat, and definitely stop by if it fits into your itinerary!

17. Spend The Day At Ocean Beach Park

Ocean Beach Park is one of Connecticut's most beautiful beaches located along the New London shoreline. Ocean Beach Park offers breathtaking views of the Atlantic Ocean, and sugar, white sand. Unique to this beach is also an Olympic style swimming pool. What makes this beach so special is that it's actually so much more than a beach. When you're visiting Ocean Beach Park, you'll also have access to a boardwalk, miniature golf course, arcade, food court, carnival rides, water slide, splash pad, playground, and nature walk. In addition to the numerous activities and attractions, the beach also hosts various events throughout the season such as: Cruise Night, Beach Blanket Movie Nights, and the Sock Hop. Parking ranges in price from about $17 to $23. Additional fees require access to the pool, miniature golf, water slides, and carnival rides. If you are visiting Connecticut between Memorial Day and Labor Day, you will definitely want to plan a day trip to Ocean Beach Park in New London.

18. Challenge Yourself At The It Adventure Ropes Course

Who would have ever thought that one of Connecticut's best ropes courses would be found inside a furniture store? Well, that is exactly where It Adventure Ropes Course is located! It Adventure Ropes Course is actually the world's largest indoor ropes course, and it's found inside Jordan's Furniture in the city of New Haven. The course contains zip lines, cargo nets, bridges, a cat walk, climbing walls, and obstacles of every nature. While battling the ropes course, you'll get to experience incredible lighting and music in the background. Even children can experience a course suited just for them at the Little It Adventure Ropes Course. When everyone is all tired out from their adventures, you can experience a water show explosion of lights, sounds, and music! If you love to be challenged and enjoy risk-taking, then you must include a trip to the It Adventure Ropes Course in New Haven.

19. Find Tranquility At Crescent Lake

Hidden in the outskirts of the small town of Southington you will find the gem that is Crescent Lake. If you enjoy outdoor activities in a scenic environment, then this is the place just for you. Crescent Lake is the perfect place to enjoy boating, kayaking, fishing, canoeing, sailing, hiking, walking, and bowhunting. Three hiking trails are available and are color coded for your convenience. You can choose a trail that best fits your capability and preference for intensity. While Crescent Lake is open all year, one of the best times to visit is during the Fall. The foliage that takes over the perimeter of the lake is remarkable. Whether you are having a light picnic or boating on the lake, the foliage that surrounds you is breathtaking.

While you're visiting Crescent Lake, you should make a stop across the street at Bradley Mountain Farm. If you're lucky, you might be able to partake in Goat Yoga! The goats of Bradley Mountain Farm and the instructors from Southington's Bloom Yoga will bring you a silly exercise class that you won't forget! Be sure to check the schedule when you're planning your Connecticut stay so that you can be sure to incorporate some Goat Yoga while enjoying Crescent Lake!

20. Pick Your Own Fruit At Lyman Orchards

Lyman Orchards, located in the town of Middlefield, is a popular destination for families all over New England. Lyman Orchards is open all year, and offers special events and foods for each season. One of the most popular activities at the orchard is picking your own crops. You can pick everything from pumpkins to strawberries and peaches. In addition, the Apple Barrel Market, contains fruits and vegetables grown directly on the Lyman property as well as various crops grown in Connecticut and local New England regions. As soon as you park and hop out of the car, the delicious aromas of fresh pies and baked delights will embrace your nostrils. A must-try is the Hi-Top Apple Pie, loaded with fresh, apple chunks and mixed with the perfect blend of spices.

Lyman Orchards isn't just known for its delectable fruits, vegetables, and baked goods. The orchard hosts several family-friendly events throughout the year that always draw visitors in from near and far. For example, the Sun Flower Maze and the Corn Maze are popular attractions for both children and adults alike. Moreover, Lyman Orchards also has its own golf center on the premises. The Jones Course, Player Course, and the Apple 9 Course each offer its own difficulty level and unique, scenic views. You can also choose to simply practice and perfect your game at the Driving Range or the Short Game Practice Area. As you are planning your Connecticut stay, be sure to research which events will be held and which crops will be in season when you are in town.

›TOURIST

"Never give up, for that is just the place and time that the tide will turn." ~ Harriet Beecher Stowe

Wisniewski

21. Devour Apple Fritters

If you happen to be visiting the state at the beginning of October, you must stop by the Apple Harvest Festival in Southington. It is a small fall fair with delicious food, fun carnival rides, and shopping tents. There is no entrance fee to attend the fair, you simply have to pay for your food and carnival rides as you go. People come from all over the state to get at least one bag of the famous apple fritters. These apple fritters are made with a secret recipe by the volunteers of Zion Lutheran Church. No matter how many times you eat these fritters, it's like a mini explosion of delicious flavor in your mouth: the perfect combination of sugar, dough, and chunks of fresh apple. You'll have to plan your timing just perfect, though, if you don't plan on waiting on a pretty, long line. The best times to purchase fritters are first thing in the morning on a weekday or during rainy weather. However, even that is not an exact science because people are always searching for these yummy delights. Some other popular food favorites are: Hot Apple Crisp, Pulled Pork Sandwiches, and Chili Bread Bowls.

In addition to the countless food options, children and adults alike will enjoy the carnival rides and games. There's also dozens of vendors selling handmade crafts, jewelry, and various arts and crafts. Also, if the weather permits, there is typically a fireworks display and a parade during the first weekend of the festival's opening, that the whole family can enjoy. During the second weekend of the festival, there is a large Arts & Crafts Fair. The Apple Harvest Festival is only open for two weekends in late September/early October. However, if you plan on visiting the state during that time period, it is highly recommended that you make a stop at this small, yet charming, fall fair.

22. Stop By The Durham Fair

The Durham Fair is another fair favorite for New Englanders near and far. The Durham Fair is held in the town of Durham over the course of one weekend at the end of September. Established in 1916, the Durham Fair is noted for being Connecticut's Largest Agricultural Fair. Much larger than the Apple Harvest Festival in Southington, the Durham Fair has everything from live music and good food, to livestock shows and exhibits. There is something for everyone, of all ages. For example, adults will enjoy the Connecticut Wine Festival and children will love the carnival games, petting zoo, and so much more. The whole family will enjoy animal pulls, motorized events, and lumber jack shows.

Due to the size of the fair, it is best to park at one of the distant lots and take the public shuttle. It is also important to know that, because the fair is only open for 3 days, it typically draws huge crowds and can be pretty congested. However, locals will tell you that it's all just part of the Durham Fair experience!

23. Observe Waterfalls

Another one of Connecticut's most beautiful state parks is Wadsworth Falls State Park in the towns of Middlefield and Middletown. This park is primarily known for the beauty of its waterfalls. The falls are distinguished as "big falls" and "little falls." The "big falls" is the area designated for viewing and observing. You'll find visitors taking photographs, enjoying picnic lunches, or simply sitting and absorbing the natural beauty that surrounds them. The "little falls" have less water pressure creating the falls, but the views are still breathtaking regardless. Trails of various levels lead into both falls. If you are not physically able to access the trails, you can park your vehicle on the opposite side of the park closer to where the "big falls" actually are. Many visitors also utilize the trails for hiking, biking, horseback riding, and pleasure walking.

While the falls are the main attraction the park, there is also a sandy beach and picnic area located opposite to the falls. This is the only area of the park where swimming is allowed. The wonderful thing about Wadsworth Falls is that it is open year round. This can be an excellent spot to enjoy a brisk, fall hike or even a snowy, winter walk. Wadsworth Falls could be a pit stop along the way of your Connecticut adventures, or it could be a fun-filled day trip. No matter the time of year, you'll find plenty to keep you mesmerized and busy at Wadsworth Falls!

24. Hike Through Sleeping Giant State Park

Sleeping Giant, located in Hamden, is another one of Connecticut's most popular state parks. This park is primarily acknowledged for its hiking trails, but the park can be utilized for much more than simply hiking. Sleeping Giant is strategically named for the form the mountaintop creates which resembles a sleeping giant. There are several hiking trails of varying levels of difficulty, with many trails crossing paths or aligning together. One of the most popular trails is the Tower Trail. This is one of the easier trails to navigate in the park because it is lined with a gravel path and is fairly level. At the top of this trail, you will find the tower or the "castle" as many visitors like to refer to it. While adults will enjoy the breathtaking views of Long Island Sound and the New Haven area from the top of the tower, children will enjoy exploring the tower, peeking out its turrets and windows.

If you are looking for a more strenuous hike, the Blue Trail is known to be one of the most difficult, if not the most difficult, trail of Sleeping Giant. You can make a daytrip out of your excursion to the park by planning a picnic lunch at one of the designated picnic areas and you can even enjoy some relaxing Trout fishing as well. Sleeping Giant is another park that is open year round, each season offering its own, unique special qualities to be seen. If your Connecticut stay leads you around the Hamden and New Haven areas, you should definitely consider stopping at Sleeping Giant.

25. Hike To Castle Craig

Castle Craig is a historical tower located atop East Peak of the Hanging Hills in Meriden. The tower is part of Hubbard Park, which sits 976 feet below the castle. Castle Craig, was originally built in 1900, and the original infrastructure, composed mostly of trap rock, still stands today. Various hiking trails cross through Hubbard Park, the most notable being a portion the Metacomet Trail. You can use these trails to explore much more than just Castle Craig. There are two main ways to get to the castle. If you prefer the hike, you must take the Blue-Blazed Trail. You can also choose to walk or drive along the paved road that leads to the castle. Once you get to the top of the peak, the views that stand before you will be breathtaking. If you're able to get into the castle and climb the stairwell to the observation deck, you'll be able to see Sleeping Giant in Hamden or even the waters of Long Island Sound.

>TOURIST

When you're finished visiting Castle Craig, you should take some time to explore Hubbard Park. One of the most common activities in the park is to feed the ducks and geese at Mirror Lake. You can also take a relaxing walk around the lake, observe the various flower gardens, and the surrounding woodlands. One of the most popular local events is held at Hubbard Park in the Spring called the Daffodil Festival. People from all over the state come together to enjoy the beautiful flowers, food good, music, and fireworks. Another one of the most popular local events is held throughout the Winter months. This is The Festival of Silver Lights. Visitors from all over visit the park to drive through and see the beautiful holiday lights and displays. It is actually a holiday tradition for many local families to visit the lights at Hubbard Park at least once during the Winter season. Whether you choose to visit the park for a quick drive through or to spend the day hiking and exploring, be sure to take some time to observe and take in the beauty of the historical Castle Craig.

26. Cruise Around The Thimble Islands

The Thimble Islands are located off the coast of the Branford shoreline at the Stony Creek Dock. The Sea Mist Thimble Islands Cruise takes passengers for a tour around the historic Thimble Islands from May through October. The Sea Mist cruise ship was specifically designed for sightseeing voyages, with comfortable seating and two-decks. Both decks can be covered and heated should the inclement weather arise. Unique to all cruise ships at the Stony Creek Dock, the Sea Mist contains the only bar on board a ship. The Sand Bar serves alcoholic beverages such as wine, beer, and rum punch. Bottled water and soda are also sold at the bar.

The Sea Mist operates on a first come, first serve basis and does not take reservations. However, private charters and dinner cruises are available by appointment. Typical tour cruising boards on the hour every hour. departs at a quarter past the hour, and lasts about 45 minutes. There are no tours after 5:00 PM as the cruise ship is then dedicated to private parties. It is important to note that credit cards are not accepted at any time, so be sure to have plenty of cash on hand!

27. Sink Into The Submarine Force Library & Museum

The Submarine Force Library & Museum, is located on the Thames River in Groton in close proximity to the Naval Submarine Base. This base is the Navy's primary submarine base on the East Coast. The Submarine Force Library & Museum contains submarine artifacts, documents, photographs, and of course, submarines! It's actually the only submarine museum that is operated directly by the United States Navy. As soon as you walk onto the property, you will see four miniature submarines. While they are considered "midget" submarines, they certainly won't seem that way when you are standing next to them!

One of the most fascinating experiences to have at the museum is exploring the USS NAUTILUS, the world's first nuclear powered submarine. Not only will you learn the history of this vintage ship, but you will also have the opportunity to see the areas where the crew worked, ate, and slept. Admission and parking into the library and museum are free. This is an educational and historical experience the whole family can enjoy. Scavenger hunts, available online or at the information desk, can help keep children involved and entertained throughout your stay as well. The Submarine Force Library & Museum is well worth a stop if you happen to be touring the New London area during your Connecticut visit.

28. Join The Animals At The Beardsley Zoo

The Beardsley Zoo, located in Bridgeport, is a Connecticut attraction that the whole family can enjoy. You will have the opportunity to observe some of North America's and South America's most exotic animals up close. Amphibians, mammals, and reptiles, oh my! There's also many species of birds and lots of tiny, crawling insects to see. In addition, the zoo protects and exhibits several endangered and threatened species such as: the Siberian tiger, the Giant anteater, and the Golden lion tamarin. Various live events are held all throughout the day as well. For instance, you can observe the River Otters and the Alligators at a live feeding session.

Be sure to check the calendar prior to your visit because the zoo is always offering new and exciting events. When you aren't busy being mesmerized and entertained by the animals, you can enjoy a snack at the Peacock Café, or if the weather permits, you can bring a picnic lunch to enjoy in the Picnic Grove. If your schedule allows, you can make a whole day out of visiting the zoo. You can also simply stop by for a couple of hours in between your other planned Connecticut adventures. Either way, kids and adults alike will be amazed by this unique, zoo experience.

29. Dining Outside At Goats N' Roses

You've probably heard of the band Guns 'N Roses. But, you probably haven't heard of the restaurant called Goats N' Roses. Goats N' Roses is located atop Carter Hill Farm in Marlborough. This special eatery offers a unique outdoor eating experience in a secluded and serene atmosphere. Goats N' Roses is notorious for its farm fresh ingredients and healthy eating options. The menu contains everything from salads and small plates to burgers and freshly made sandwiches. Make sure that you don't fill up too much on all of the delicious food, because you have to save room for some ice cream. The Goats N' Roses staff puts together ice cream creations fresh to order, just for you.

Since the restaurant is an outdoor eatery, it does operate according to the weather. It is also important to note that the restaurant only accepts cash. If you're looking for a different kind of eating experience in a quiet and natural atmosphere, then its highly suggested you incorporate a visit to Goats N' Roses during your Connecticut trip!

30. Eat Pizza at Pepe's

While Connecticut is not necessarily known for its amazing pizza, Frank Pepe's of New Haven is definitely known for its pizza. Yes, there are many other Pepe's locations around Connecticut and a select few in bordering states, but there is none other like the original Franke Pepe's in New Haven. The pizza is so incredible and so popular that they had to open additional locations in various areas around the state.

Pepe's pizza is some of Connecticut's oldest pizza, dating back all the way to the 1920's. There's just nothing else like Pepe's mouthwatering tomato sauce and fresh mozzarella cheese baked on a handmade crust in a woodfired, brick oven. If you're already out and about having adventures in New Haven County, you must stop by and have a least one slice of pizza at the original Frank Pepe's Pizza.

"The heart should be cultivated with more assiduity than the head."

~ Noah Webster

Wisniewski

31. Explore Exotic Animals At Action Wildlife

Action Wildlife sits in the quiet, rolling hills of Northwestern Connecticut in a little town called Goshen. At Action Wildlife adults and children have the opportunity to observe, interact with, and learn about animals from not only North America, but from Africa, India, New Zealand, Asia, and the Arctic. You can even observe the animals up close through the drive-thru safari exhibit. At the petting zoo area, children will enjoy mingling with, feeding, and touching the smaller animal species.

While the exotic animals are the main attraction at the zoo, there is also a museum and a hands-on exploration center where visitors can learn more about each of the animal species in their natural habitats. After you enjoy a day with the animals, you can have a leisurely lunch under the pavilion located at the back of the museum.

Action Wildlife operates on a seasonal schedule and is typically open from the beginning of Summer to the beginning of Fall. If

Action Wildlife is something you would like to incorporate into your Connecticut visit, then it is recommended that you plan accordingly.

32. Tour the Capitol Building

Of course you really can't visit the state of Connecticut without visiting its capital in the city of Hartford. The Capitol Building and Bushnell Park offer a look into the history of Hartford as well as the state of Connecticut. Both places are located in the city of Hartford. Bushnell Park is actually situated right down the hill from the state's Capitol building. It's impossible to miss the golden dome protruding from the Capitol. The Capitol Building is open for guided and self-guided tours throughout the week. These tours will provide insight into the state's history as well as its legislative process. If the House and Senate are in session, you'll have the opportunity to observe the proceedings from the public galleries. During your tour, you'll also visit the Hall of Flags and the Connecticut Hall of Fame. Your tour and education of the Capitol wouldn't be complete without walking down the hill to Bushnell Park.

33. Stroll Through Bushnell Park

Bushnell Park, located down the hill from the Capitol Building, is rich in both beauty and historical significance. As you enter the park, you'll notice the well landscaped grassy fields, the playing fields, and a beautiful lake where a large, flowing fountain marks its center. These areas are frequently accessed by local residents and people working in Hartford for picnics, walks in the park, or to simply relax in nature for a while. If you are visiting during the Fall, Spring, or Summer, be sure to visit the Carousel in the park. This wooden Carousel is a true mark of history and beauty, dating back all the way to the early 1900s. In the Winter, the park also contains an ice skating rink. In addition, the park is home to countless rare and native varieties of trees such as the Japanese Pagoda and the Gingko Tree.

Aside from the park's obvious beauty, the park holds historical significance as well. The Soldiers & Sailors Memorial Arch is a miraculous landmark that can only truly be appreciated from up close and inside. Tours of the Arch run periodically throughout the week, so be sure to check the touring schedule in advance. In addition to touring the Soldiers & Sailors Memorial Arch, you can also partake in a guided historical tour of the entire park. This will lead you through the park's statues, war memorials, native trees, the Carousel, and the Performance Pavilion. A guided tour with a trained guide is probably the best way to get the most out of this experience.

Whether you visit Bushnell Park for its educational and historical value or simply to relish in its beauty, its really a necessary experience for any Connecticut tourist. Bushnell Park hosts numerous events throughout the year as well, so be sure to keep yourself up-to-date with what will be happening when you are in town.

34. Shopping, Walking, And Eating At West Hartford Center

West Hartford is a quaint town located in Central Connecticut. West Hartford Center is the area of town known to be bustling with dozens of shops and restaurants. It is the perfect place to spend a romantic evening or a day of shopping and walking. West Hartford Center contains shops and restaurants lined along both sides of the Farmington Avenue, La Salle Road, North Main Street, and South Main Street. The restaurants in this area serve everything from seafood to Italian and Japanese. No matter what your palate is craving, chances are you will find something to satisfy it when visiting West Hartford Center. This, of course, includes delectable desserts! Ben & Jerry's Ice Cream and Milkcraft are two of the most popular places for ice cream and milkshakes. Just walking in the vicinity of these two shops will make your mouth salivate as the aromas of chocolate and fresh made ice cream waft through your nose.

    Also popular to West Hartford Center are the many bars serving up unique beverages in fun and charming atmospheres. For example, you can have drinks on the rooftop of the Elbow Room when the weather is nice or you can sit on the outdoor patio to enjoy tacos and margaritas at Bar Taco. When you're not busy eating or drinking, you can take the time to peruse the various little shops located throughout the center. These shops have everything from clothing and jewelry to antiques and toys. West Hartford is one of the most popular attractions located in Central Connecticut, so be sure to stop by at least once during your stay.

35. Lodging And Relaxing At The Madison Beach Hotel

The Madison Beach Hotel not only serves as an elegant and luxurious place of lodging, but it also contains a wonderful restaurant, a stunning, private beach, and is in close proximity to downtown Madison. Most people believe that beaches serve their best purpose in Summer. However, the beach can really be just as beautiful in the Winter. One of the accommodations inside the Madison Beach Hotel that is open to the public is The Porch, located inside The Wharf Restaurant. When the weather permits, visitors can enjoy dining on the outside patio which overlooks the private beach and Long Island Sound. When the weather isn't ideal, a plastic screen protects visitors from the outdoor elements. The Porch is also heated during the colder months. The Porch is the perfect spot to enjoy some appetizers and drinks while watching the sun cascade over the sound.

    For those that prefer indoor dining, The Wharf Restaurant is an elegant, yet casual place to enjoy good company, delicious food, and a charming atmosphere. In the Summer, the hotel hosts The Grassy Strip Music & Art Series, which is also open to the public. Families are welcome to enjoy free entertainment on the grassy terrain that lies between the beach and the hotel. If you are just stopping by the hotel for the view, you can travel not far down the road to Downtown Madison where you can explore shops, restaurants, boutiques, and an old-fashioned live theater. However, if your wallet permits it, you won't regret spending the extra dollar to lodge at this shore side hotel.

36. Rejuvinate At The Water's Edge Resort and Spa

The Water's Edge Resort and Spa is one of Connecticut's most famous, luxurious hotels located directly on the shoreline. It is a popular destination for both locals and tourists for vacationing, weekend getaways, romantic escapes, spa relaxation, and fine dining. Moreover, the hotel also hosts various events throughout the year that are open to the public. The Sunday Brunch Buffet is definitely a local favorite.

The Royal Water-view Suite, the Three-Bedroom Suite, and the Ocean Front Villas By The Sea are some of the most elegant, spacious, and beautiful lodging rooms found anywhere in the state of Connecticut. However, these rooms are incredibly popular and book up well in advance. If you consider staying in one of this rooms during your trip, be sure to place your reservation as soon as possible.

Even if you are not staying at the hotel, you can enjoy several of the wonderful and serene experiences offered by the hotel. For example, The Spa at Water's Edge is open all year, and visitors come from all over to partake in this unique, spa experience. The spa offers everything from nail treatments and body waxing to massages and full body wraps. Whether you choose to come in for a simple pedicure or to spend the entire day at the spa, you are guaranteed to leave feeling refreshed, relaxed, and rejuvenated.

37. Have Fun At The Hops Company

If you like to have a good time and you like to drink beer, then you need to consider visiting The Hops Company in Derby at some point during your Connecticut stay. While The Hops Company is not considered a brewery, it carries over 40 craft beers. For those that are not big beer drinkers, THC also serves ciders, cocktails, and wine. Unlike typical breweries or vineyards, The Hops Company serves its own food as well. They are well known for their delicious, fresh pizza, but also serve appetizers, salads, and snacks.

When the weather permits, the best place to enjoy yourself is on the outdoor bar and beer garden. In the spacious beer garden, you will find a great variety of lawn games such as: Giant Jenga, Cornhole, and Darts. Even when the weather is not favorable, you can play indoor board games or relax by the cozy fireplace.

Throughout the week, THC hosts events such as trivia and live music. The Hops Company is the perfect place to stop to have a casual, fun, and carefree time while exploring Connecticut.

38. Drink Beer At Stony Creek Brewery

    Connecticut is home to numerous breweries located in various locations throughout the state. As the popularity for craft beer grows, so too do the craft breweries themselves. The Stony Creek Brewery is one such brewery found on the Branford waterfront. The brewery contains waterfront seating on lawn chairs and picnic tables situated on gravel laid grounds. Seating around a couple of outdoor fireplaces is also available in this area. In addition, games such as Corn Hole are placed around the outdoor seating. An outside patio with tables and chairs is located directly behind the lower waterfront seating. An additional upper deck patio sits above this patio as well. The indoor taproom is just as beautiful as spacious as the available outdoor seating.

    Throughout the year, various food trucks will park outside the brewery for your eating pleasure. For example, Lenny & Joe's Fish Cocktail and Taco Pacifico are two of the food trucks that have previously stopped by. The brewery does not serve food other than the food trucks that may be on hand. As a result, you are welcome to bring in your own snacks and food platters. Also, several takeout menus are available should you wish to order food for delivery.

Children are welcome into the brewery, but must be accompanied with an adult at all times. At various dates throughout the year, the brewery also hosts events and live music. The Stony Creek Brewery would be an excellent place to stop while visiting the greater New Haven County.

39. Visit The Mark Twain House And Museum

Connecticut is proud to be the home to one of the nation's most historical landmarks, The Mark Twain House and Museum. Located in the city of Hartford, The Mark Twain House and Museum was the home of author Samuel

Clemens, better known as Mark Twain, and his family. It is hard not to be fascinated by the vintage architecture with which the building was constructed. Now a museum, visitors have the opportunity to explore this 25 room building, seeing up close the places where Twain wrote some of his most famous works.

    While the guided tours are the most popular, you can also spice things up a bit by trying a Living History Tour, a Graveyard Shift Ghost Tour, or a Clue Tour. In addition, the museum is masterfully decorated during the holiday season. The Mark Twain House and Museum is open all year, but hosts numerous events as well, so be sure to check in prior to your trip to see what exciting things will be happening!

40. Go Back In Time At The Dinosaur State Park

It's hard to find museums that can truly bring you back to the age of dinosaurs. The Dinosaur State Park, located in Rocky Hill, is one of the largest, actual dinosaur track sites in all of North America. At this museum, you'll be able to personally see fossil tracks that date back to the Jurassic Period, over 200 million years ago! Not only does the museum contain real dinosaur tracks and fossils, but it's also recreated dinosaur models and dioramas, eluding to a peek into what life was like during the age of the dinosaurs.

In addition to the museum exhibits, two miles of nature trails traverse through the surrounding land. As you walk the trails, you'll be able to explore a variety of habitats, plants, and animals in their natural surroundings. At the Aboretum, which is outside near the nature trails, you'll be able to observe a series of plants that existed during the earliest dinosaur ages.

Children will be fascinated by The Dinosaur State Park, as they are offered the experience to go back in time, envisioning what life was like for the dinosaurs. With that being said, adults who have an interest in dinosaur history will find just as much magic and fun as children. The museum is open year round, so you can choose to stop by no matter when you are visit Connecticut.

"Patriotism is supporting your country all the time, and your government when it deserves it." ~ Mark Twain

Wisniewski

41. Walk The West Cornwall Covered Bridge

The West Cornwall Covered Bridge is one of the few covered bridges left standing in the state of Connecticut. You'll find this historic landmark tucked away in the town of West Cornwall crossing the Housatonic River. While the bridge has undergone some structural modifications since its construction in the 1860s, the majority of the original bridge remain intact. The bridge is actually still in service, carrying traffic over the Housatonic River to Connecticut Route 128.

The architecture of the bridge is absolutely breathtaking. The outside of the bridge is a deep red hue, with intricately placed windows along the sides. On the inside, you can see the wooden lattices connecting the red spruce wooden bars which remain held together by treenails.

While you are able to drive over the bridge, the best views to be had are while walking underneath and through the bridge. The bridge is just as beautiful in Winter and

Summer as it is in Spring and Fall. If your Connecticut trip takes you through the Litchfield County, be sure to incorporate a stop at the West Cornwall Covered Bridge.

42. Dining at Fresh Salt at Saybrook Point Inn

Fresh Salt is an upscale restaurant located inside the Saybrook Point Inn & Spa. Located on the water, the restaurant offers spectacular views of where the Connecticut River meets Long Island Sound. The restaurant is well known for its use of fresh and local ingredients, especially those in the seafood dishes. This would be the perfect location for a romantic evening dinner or a scenic happy hour of cocktails and appetizers. However, the restaurant does offer a children's menu for those dining with kids. One of the most popular attractions at Fresh Salt is its Sunday Brunch. The Sunday Brunch serves an extensive buffet including everything from fruit and waffles to shrimp cocktail and salmon. The Saybrook Inn & Spa is an additional option for lodging, if you would like to stay in a more elite hotel along the Connecticut shoreline.

43. Eat Gourmet Burgers And Hot Dogs Like A Local

Riley's Hot Dog & Burger Gourmet is a local favorite. Riley's originally started as a hot dog cart on South Street in the city of New Britain in 2010. However, due to its overwhelming popularity, the hot dog cart has now grown to a little burger shop located on Glen Street in New Britain. Riley's focuses on creating hot dog and burger masterpieces using local and fresh ingredients, family recipes, and unique toppings.

Some examples of the gourmet hot dogs that you'll find at Riley's are: The Junkyard Dog and The Loco Taco Dog. The Mac & Cheese Burger and The Magical Mushroom & Swiss Burger are two of the special, gourmet burgers that

Riley's serves up. Riley's Hot Dog & Burger Gourmet is the perfect place to stop for lunch or dinner while you're exploring Central Connecticut.

44. Walk The Labyrinths

Chances are, you will be planning as much into your visit to Connecticut as possible. If you're visiting Connecticut on a vacation, it may not seem like much of a vacation with all the running about that you'll be doing, going from one place to the next. Walking a labyrinth is an excellent opportunity to relax, slow down, and re-center yourself. No matter your religious background, walking a labyrinth is a spiritual and rejuvenating experience.

While a handful of labyrinths are located throughout the state, there are two in particular that offer special atmospheres. The first is the Labyrinth at The Holy Family Passionist Retreat Center in West Hartford, which is open to the public at any time. This Labyrinth is strategically located behind the Retreat Center in a serene, wooded setting. As you walk the Labyrinth amongst the trees, birds chirping, and sun shining, its impossible not to have a feeling of calmness and peace.

  The second labyrinth is located at The Mercy By The Sea Retreat and Conference Center in Madison. Sitting next to Long Island Sound, this labyrinth is guaranteed to give you a sense of quiet and stillness as the waves are crashing in the background.

    It is highly suggested that you consider incorporating a labyrinth walk into your Connecticut visit. If you're exploring the shoreline, the Madison labyrinth is probably more convenient; whereas, if you are spending time in the Central Connecticut area, the West Hartford labyrinth would be better suited for you. Either way, walking the labyrinth will help you to slow down and take some time to appreciate the little things.

45. Eat, Stay, Explore At Hopkins Inn

Hopkins Inn is a charming and historic inn located in the Litchfield Hills in the town of Warren. Sitting on the northern shore of Lake Waramaug, Hopkins Inn is just as beautiful a place to lodge as it is to enjoy a peaceful meal and relax. The inn only has twelve guest rooms and two apartments that are open for lodging year round. The majority of the rooms have a remarkable lakeside view. Additionally, guests who are lodging at the inn also have access to the lake and Hopkins Inn beach, located a short distance from the inn itself.

If you are just stopping by the inn to relish in its beauty and food, you won't be disappointed. The restaurant is well known for its unique, Austrian cuisine. However, the restaurant has recently added more American food options to its menu as well. When dining inside, the tall, glass windows allow stunning views of Lake Waramaug. When the weather permits, you have the choice to dine on the outside terrace.

The downfall is that the restaurant is only open from late March to the beginning of January. When the restaurant is closed, Hopkins Inn operates as a simple bed and breakfast. Therefore, if you weren't planning on staying at the inn, but desired to eat at the restaurant, you'll have to plan accordingly. Hopkins Inn does serve as an excellent place to stop while visiting and exploring the greater Litchfield Hills area.

46. Dine At Apricot's Restaurant and Pub

Apricot's Restaurant and Pub is a scenic eatery found on the banks of the Farmington River in the town of Farmington. The building with which Apricot's occupies actually served as a trolley barn in the early 1800s. The "restaurant" portion of the building is found on the second floor and is considered to be more suited for a fine dining experience. Guests have two dining rooms to choose from when desiring a more elegant atmosphere. The "pub" portion of the building is on the first level, offering a more casual dining experience. On the menu, you'll find everything from Mussels and Shrimp Cocktail to a Pan Seared Crispy Panko Chicken Francaise.

Perhaps one of the most popular attractions at the restaurant is its outdoor patio, allowing guests the opportunity to dine on the banks of the Farmington River. It is truly a special experience to enjoy your food and drink as the sounds and sights of the Farmington River stream along in front of you. Apricot's is open all year, and is the perfect place to stop and enjoy a meal while exploring Central Connecticut.

47. Drink, Eat, Relax On The Roof

A quality rooftop dining experience is hard to come by. However, Rooftop 120 in Glastonbury is one of New England's largest rooftops that is open year round. With outdoor heaters and two firepits, guests have no problem staying warm on colder days and nights. At Rooftop 120, you'll enjoy a casual and fun atmosphere while overlooking the greater Hartford area. The drink menu offers a wide variety of cocktails, wine, beer, and martinis. In addition, guests can also order small plates and food entrees. During the weekday afternoons, Rooftop 120 also hosts various Happy Hour specials.

If you are looking for a more intimate and elegant experience, Rooftop 120 has also opened a restaurant called Nosh 120. The dining room atmosphere is perfect for a romantic evening, a girls' night, or for special occasions. On this menu, you'll find everything from Oysters and Salads to

Seafood Ravioli and Pomegranate Glazed Salmon. Specialty cocktails, martinis, wine, and beer are also available on the Tosh 120 Menu. If you're looking for a fun and unique experience while visiting the greater Hartford area, you should consider stopping by Rooftop 120 and/or Tosh 120 in Glastonbury.

48. Watch And Dine At 121 Restaurant At OXC

Do you enjoy watching airplanes take off and land at the airport? Do you find this to be a mesmerizing and even relaxing experience? 121 Restaurant offers a unique dining experience as it is located directly across from the runways and taxi-ways at Oxford Airport. As you are eating, drinking, and talking, you can also be watching small jets taking off and landing.

Though the views are primarily what attracts guests to this restaurant, the restaurant is also known for using organic ingredients and sustainable materials. As a result, guests are always ensured the freshest quality of food. The Lunch and Dinner Menu offers everything from Salads and Appetizers to Pizza and Entrees. A Kid's Menu is also available. 121 also provides a drink menu containing Wine, Beer, and Champagne. 121 Restaurant is a great location to stop, relax, and enjoy a fun view while you are visiting New Haven County.

49. Drink, Party, And Pedal On The Elm City Park Bike

The Elm City Party Bike is New England's first party bike that offers fun, partying, and pedaling. What's better than exercising while bar hopping? Local residents and tourists are fascinated by this unique, biking experience. The bike will take you on a tour of the city of New Haven, bringing you through some of the state's most beautiful architecture, historical landmarks, and colleges. Of course you'll also stop by the city's most popular restaurants, bars, and stores.

As a guest on the bike, you will have a trained driver who steers while you do the pedaling. The Elm City Party Bike offers a variety of Private Tours. You can book a Historic Narrated Tour or a Spirits, Spirit, & Experience Tour with a ghost finder and certified medium! You can also simply buy a ticket and join a two-hour Group Tour. A Cocktail Spin Class is even available! Riding along the Elm City Party Bike is the best way to soak in some history, get some exercise, and have fun, all at the same time!

50. Look Forward To Seeing You

Now that you have an idea of not only the best places in Connecticut to visit as a tourist, but also as a local, it's time to plan your trip! Remember, Connecticut is small, so plan your trip accordingly. Try to visit places that are located in a similar area so that you can get the most "bang for your buck." For example, create an itinerary that allows you to visit several places in Central Connecticut on the same day. As a four season state, Connecticut has unique qualities that make each time of the year special and different. While you can visit Connecticut at any time, keep in mind that certain events, such as fall festivals, only occur during specific seasons. As a result, be sure to plan your trip in advance based on what you would like to do, where you would like to go, and when you would like to do it. No matter when you visit, be sure to relax, take a step back, and enjoy yourself. You'll be happy you did!

Wisniewski

Top Reasons to Book This Trip

- **Weather**: With the changing seasons, each time of the year offers its own, unique characteristics.
- **Size**: Connecticut is small, so you can visit a lot of places in a short period of time.
- **Variety**: There is so much to do, see, eat, and explore.

Wisniewski

> TOURIST

GREATER THAN A TOURIST

Visit GreaterThanATourist.com
http://GreaterThanATourist.com

Sign up for the Greater Than a Tourist Newsletter
http://eepurl.com/cxspyf

Follow us on Facebook:
https://www.facebook.com/GreaterThanATourist

Follow us on Pinterest:
http://pinterest.com/GreaterThanATourist

Follow us on Instagram:
http://Instagram.com/GreaterThanATourist

Wisniewski

> TOURIST

GREATER THAN A TOURIST

Please leave your honest review of this book on Amazon and Goodreads. Thank you.

We appreciate your positive and negative feedback as we try to provide tourist guidance in their next trip from a local.

> TOURIST

GREATER THAN A TOURIST

Our Story

Traveling is a passion of the "Greater than a Tourist" series creator. Lisa studied abroad in college, and for their honeymoon Lisa and her husband toured Europe. During her travels to Malta, an older man tried to give her some advice based on his own experience living on the island since he was a young boy. She was not sure if she should talk to the stranger but was interested in his advice. When traveling to some places she was wary to talk to locals because she was afraid that they weren't being genuine. Through her travels, Lisa learned how much locals had to share with tourists. Lisa created the "Greater Than a Tourist" book series to help connect people with locals. A topic that locals are very passionate about sharing.

Wisniewski

\>TOURIST

\> TOURIST

GREATER THAN A TOURIST

Notes

Printed in Great Britain
by Amazon